MW00946423

RISE

and

SHINE

CHRISTIAN S. BROWN

RISE

and

SHINE

30 Daily Devotionals for Self-Empowerment in Christ

Christian S. Brown

CHRISTIAN S. BROWN

Copyright © 2016 Christian Brown

All rights reserved.

All rights reserved. Except as permitted under the U.S. Copyright Act of 1976, this publication shall not be broadcast, rewritten, distributed, or transmitted without prior written permission from the author.

THE HOLY BIBLE, NEW INTERNATIONAL VERSION®, NIV® Copyright © 1973, 1978, 1984, 2011 by Biblica, Inc. ™ Used by permission. All rights reserved worldwide.

ISBN-13: **978-1541324374**

RISE AND SHINE

RISE AND SHINE

Contents

Vii   **Introduction**

1   **Opening Prayer**

1   **Day 1**: "Making Time for God"

5   **Day 2**: "Be Still"

9   **Day 3**: "Standing on Scripture"

13   **Day 4**: "The Divine Direction"

17   **Day 5**: "No Stressing and Praying"

21   **Day 6**: "You are Somebody"

25   **Day 7**: "Waking up Your Dreams"

29   **Day 8**: "Beyond the Fear of Failure"

33   **Day 9**: "Small Things Matter"

37   **Day 10**: "Write it Down"

41   **Day 11**: "The Prayerful Leader"

45   **Day 12**: "Uncrushable"

49   **Day 13**: "Stand"

53   **Day 14**: "Trust God Even When You Can't Trace God"

57   **Day 15**: "Staying in Character"

61   **Day 16:**   "Praise Through Your Pain"

65   **Day 17:**   "Forgiveness"

69   **Day 18:**   "Free from Fear"

73   **Day 19:**   "Agape Love"

77   **Day 20:**   "Relationships"

81   **Day 21:**   "Waiting for the Appointed Time"

85   **Day 22:**   "Turning the Other Cheek"

89   **Day 23:**   "Show Up"

93   **Day 24:**   "Increased Attacks"

97   **Day 25:**   "The Power of Words"

101   **Day 26:**   "Things Change"

105   **Day 27:**   "Stay Focused"

109   **Day 28:**   "A Divine Interruption"

113   **Day 29:**   " Praise God in Advance"

117   **Day 30:**   "The Shepherd's Voice"

121   **Personal Prayers Section**

RISE AND SHINE

CHRISTIAN S. BROWN

DEDICATION

This book is dedicated to the four fearless women who have shaped me into the woman I have become. Thank you to Janice, Tamera, Enchantra, and Sharon.

RISE AND SHINE

FOREWORD

"Once you have a true, authentic, unscripted, one on one encounter with God it will leave a residue. If there's no residue then you did not have an experience with God, you only had a moment."

- Tamera Brown

This book will lead you to have multiple experiences with our Lord and Savior. The author has truly allowed God to speak through her in order to bring healing and closure to anyone who takes the time to embrace the wisdom and revelation that has been revealed in this amazing devotional book. She has gone beneath the surface of life's most complex and painful challenges in order to expose it through prayer and wisdom.

It is obvious that Christian has allowed us to see into private moments of hurt, confusion and vulnerability so that the voice of God could be heard and the glory of God could be seen in each and every devotional.

Allow her experiences and discernment to help introduce you to a new way of thinking, believing, and living. As you journey through this devotional, it will aid you to illuminate the divine purposes and plans that God has for each and every one of its readers. Christian is more than an author. She is a selfless, bold, and fearless soldier who God has equipped for such a time as this. May you be blessed in your reading as you are inspired to RISE above your obstacles and SHINE the light of God in all that you do.

Your mother,
Minister Tamera Brown

RISE AND SHINE

Introduction

We all can share a story or testimony that may bring you to your knees. I've discovered with time that it is not about what you go through, but the mindset that you have in the midst of struggle, that determines the outcome. I know all too well the various stressors of life and I have overcome them all through being victorious in my devotional time with God.

No matter the happenings of life around you; no matter the defeat that the Enemy may assault you with; no matter the hardships that you, your family, your church, and your world may face, we are to remember that all things are possible when we cast our cares upon Jesus. In the world, it is essential that we spend daily moments with God so that we may rise above any obstacle that may be encountered. We are to rise daily, in mind, body, and spirit and I pray that this devotional book is a tool to assist you in this holistic, empowering journey in Christ. RISE in relationship with God.

In the story of Jesus, we are often reminded of the crucifixion. We are reminded of the nails that were driven in His feet and hands and how He hung on the cross for all to see. Jesus preached to the masses, healed the blind, and empowered those in oppression, only to endure the most horrific death that one could encounter. Despite all, I am so glad that the story of Jesus does not end there, because on the third day, He rose from the grave with all power in His hands.

Just like Jesus, many of us have been spiritually attacked at some point in our life. Some days we look at our past, present, and future and believe that life has defeated us over and over again. Yet on other days we are happy, optimistic, and joyous in the Lord and we feel that we can conquer the world. No matter the season of life that you may find yourself in, I pray that you will be encouraged, empowered, and inspired in the Lord. Instead of focusing on the crosses that we must bear, instead of putting the emphasis on pain or tribulation, I pray that you are encouraged to endure it all so that you may RISE above, just as Jesus demonstrated for us when He rose. You too, can rise in empowerment through Christ and may these devotionals serve as a tool to address the many issues of our lives.

As you journey with Jesus during these precious moments with God, I pray that you develop a risen spirit to overcome any obstacle that may serve as a hindrance to your growth. I am declaring that you will RISE in faith, RISE in purpose, RISE in love, and RISE in holistic empowerment. Life is unfair in many ways as the Enemy seeks to destroy us with hopelessness. But today, I pray that you remember the power within that God has already provided you. No longer will you engage life with a defeated and crucified spirit. Instead you will be like Jesus, rising above defeat with victory.

This devotional book will transcend all races, statuses, creeds and nationalities, encouraging all to become better followers of Christ- starting from within. I pray that you become inspired in your personal walk with the Lord, and that you allow your light to shine both near and far for all to see. You have places to journey and more of the world to witness, so RISE, dream, and pursue all that the Lord has for you.

Let's begin this spiritual journey together. Let's RISE above adversity. Let's SHINE in Christ.

Opening Prayer

"I Will Follow You"

Lord, if You lead me, I will follow. Psalm 119:105 declares that, "Your word is a lamp for my feet, a light unto my path," so I ask that You guide the path on which I journey, today and forevermore. Without Your navigation, I am lost and in need of Your direction. I ask that You take my hands and my heart, and guide me along the way. I understand that in order for me to fully comprehend the depth of Your leadership, I must be obedient in following Your will and Your way, even when the destination is uncertain. I must trust Your navigation over my own. Please grant me the desire and obedience to be guided by You without resistance, Lord.

The unknowns of my life represent the beauty of my faith in You. Order my steps, O Lord. Lead and guide me every step of the way. I ask that I not get distracted by the pace at which I am walking, but that I stay focused on completing the journey itself. I will follow You as You lead me away from dangers and into my destiny; as You lead me closer to victories and away from defeats; as You lead me away from fears into fearlessness.

When I am unable to walk any longer, I trust that You will pick me up and carry me. When the path is filled with darkness and I struggle to see what lies ahead, I will trust Your guiding light to lead me to the places that You have for me. I know You will protect and shield me, God. I thank You for loving me enough to lead me. Thank You for being the light that shines through the rain, sleet, or snow, for Your guidance is everlasting. Amen.

RISE AND SHINE

Day 1

"Making Time for God"

Scripture: James 4:8

When you are in a crisis, in need of answers or desiring the presence of God, what if God used the phrase "I'm too busy." We would feel neglected and abandoned by the One who promises to be there for us through all moments. I am afraid that too often we use this very same phrase toward God unapologetically. We wake up and go throughout our routine without giving God the time that He deserves. We live in a world consumed by the notion that the busier you are, the better you are, but we should not fill up our lives with so much clutter that we are too busy to rest in the presence of God. Our spiritual growth and time with God should never be secondary to other routines of life, for He is a jealous God.

You make time for what is important to you. You participate in your favorite hobbies, check social media, converse with various friends, and many more things throughout your day. Is God included? God should be the most important to us. Therefore we must intentionally make time for spiritual growth and relationship with God. He is not asking for your entire day; only a second, minute, or hour of your time.

Time with God is a necessity to the nourishment of the soul. It makes us stronger, wiser, and more capable to endure the hassles of daily life. If you notice that you feel distant from God and the plans He has for you, I encourage you to spend time in His company. The attacks of the Enemy are strongest when we are the furthest away from the presence of the Lord. So today, I pray that you find moments throughout your day where you can talk to God. Whisper a prayer, give thanks, and let your light shine for His glory.

Our priorities are a reflection of our very being. If you prioritize things or people before God, know that your spiritual growth and future is not a priority either. Free yourself from the busyness of life and make time for what is important. Strengthening your relationship with God first will give you the power to care for your family, relationships, job, school, and your purpose. The Word of the Lord declares in James 4:8: "Come near to God, and He will come near to you." Never stray away from the source that gives you energy for life. Today, I declare for you to feed your spirit and soul by making God essential. Get close to God in the ways that you feel the Holy Spirit the most. It may be prayer, fasting, writing, meditating, singing or any other spiritual discipline. Find what works for you today and do not fear the nearness of the Holy Spirit.

Prayer: Lord, do not let me get sidetracked by the busyness of my routine. I desire to grow closer to You daily; not just in my time of need, but every day of my life. Help me to see that You should be first in my life. Allow me to seek freedom from distractions so that I may spend time with You daily. Strengthen me and my presence with You, dear Lord. Amen.

Day 2

"Be Still"

Scripture: Psalm 46:10

Some of us are taught that faith without works is dead, so we correlate inaction with laziness and wasted time. Due to this idea, we spend most of our days not living in the moment of now, but dreaming, planning, and organizing for the days, weeks, and months to come. Have you ever been in a place where you have spent so much time trying to figure out "what's next" that you frustratingly start to question the mission and the path in which you are headed?

The world has made us believe that the busier we are, the more we possess power, status, and authority. But in truth, God requires less action and more faith sometimes in our lives. Let me be clear that I am not telling you that action is unnecessary to be obedient to God. I am simply saying that in order for us to act and know where God is directing us, we need to know that if we sit still and listen faithfully for God, He will show up. Today, I ask that you stop planning endlessly for what is forthcoming, but that you will be still, so that you may hear from the Lord.

The Word of God in Psalm 46:10 declares to, "Be still and know that I am God." For many of us who like to be in control of things, this is a very daunting task. After all, your plan and execution is better than the Lord's, right? No! Sometimes we are so busy telling God our visions for life that we drown out His voice, unable to hear His guidance because our voices are so loud. Be still!

Today, I challenge you to slow down your "I have to save the world" heart, and your "what's next?" mindset because your ways are not God's ways. We often lead God in our lives instead of allowing God to lead us. I know that He has given you a vision for your business, education, nonprofit, family, book, or other adventure of life, but if you are not guided by the Holy Spirit, you will burn out and eventually the mission will miss out as well. You must learn to follow before you can lead. Follow God and then watch Him cultivate your leadership and future.

When you are still, be intentional about tuning out the noises of your life. It can be people, places, distractions, or simply the inner voices telling you that you are not capable of achieving more. Remember in 2 Timothy 1:7: "God did not give you a spirit of fear," so be bold in your stillness. In your silence, I ask that you increase your prayers and meditation to God. Get into the Word and seek the face of the Lord.

Remember to be led by the Holy Spirit as you matriculate through various stages and seasons of your life. If God does not say do it, or your spirit is not at peace, you need to be still and get further direction before moving forward. Once God gives you direction to move beyond that stillness, remember you are to uphold the vision with integrity and selflessness. It is not about you because you are only a tool to get others closer to God. God is calling up leaders, and you are one of them. Yes, you! So follow the lead of the Holy Spirit and not the motives of your own will.

Prayer: Lord, I ask that You allow me to sit still and slow down. Free me from concerns about planning what's next and allow me to see the greatness of now. Holy Spirit, lead and guide me when it is time to move, so that I am doing Your will and not my own. Break me from the fear of rest and standing still. Rejuvenate me, Lord. Replenish my excitement to be led by You. Amen.

RISE AND SHINE

Day 3

"Standing on Scripture"

Scripture: *1 Corinthians 15:58*

Simply knowing scripture does not make you a believer and follower of Christ. Although quoting it may be impressive to those around you in particular settings, it unfortunately does not earn you any brownie points with God. God is more concerned with the condition of your heart while living out the Word rather than memorizing it. You are to harbor the Word of God in your spirit, for it will serve as a great tool to shift hearts, minds, and souls. Just imagine you are having a bad day, and just as you feel as if all things are falling apart, you begin quoting Philippians 4:13: " I can do all things through Christ who strengthens me." The Scripture will not only encourage your mind to endure, but will also influence your spirit and your surrounding environment. Speaking life into the atmosphere is contagious, so I pray that today, you begin to fight all things not merely through emotions or intellect, but that you fight it using the tools from Scripture.

As a believer, God does not promise us perfect days. Life experience teaches us that there are some occurrences we absolutely do not have the power to control. It may be an outcome on an exam, a relationship that you tried very hard to mend, the direction of your life, the birth of children, marriage troubles, a financial deficit, or any other issue that you may find yourself unable to escape at the moment. While in the various battles that you are faced with, know that God has given you the tools and armor to fight. You must stand on Scripture that points you to Christ, the foundation of your very existence. I pray today that you refuse to settle on bad news or that you see beyond the walls that have been built around you to keep you isolated. I pray that you break through the negativity by speaking positively over your life and the lives of others. Your children, family, friends, or community need you. Learn to stand on Scripture, speak boldly into the atmosphere, and know that God hears all.

Why should you stand on Scripture? Great question! Always remember that there is no occurrence you can experience that has not been addressed in God's Word. I pray that you keep an arsenal of Scripture in your spirit so that when the Enemy comes your way, you can defeat his schemes with the Word of God. Start off small; try learning a little Scripture at a time. God is not impressed at the number of scriptures you recite from your head. He is more interested in knowing that it is embedded in your heart. Next time you feel attacked on your job, in your relationship, in your confidence, or in your happiness, just know that God has already spoken life into that situation. Allow the Word to be your foundation and if you stand boldly on its promises, you surely will not fall. Do not fight your battles alone. Let the Word of God do it for you.

Prayer: Dear Lord, I ask that today, I keep Scripture in my personal arsenal to fight the Enemy and negativity in the world. I will no longer feel defeated. I will shift my mindset to speak life despite what is around me. Lord, please guide me and allow me to stand on Your Word all the days of my life. In Your name I do pray. Amen.

Day 4

"The Divine Direction"

Scripture: Psalm 119:133

Most of us know the directions to our homes, jobs, schools, grocery stores and many other essential locations. We can find ourselves going to these various places free of assistance from maps or technology because the journey is embedded in our memory.

So what happens when you are asked the directions of your life? Where are you heading and how will you get there? Knowing this answer too soon or failing to know it at all can discourage people and they then find themselves stagnant, afraid to move. On the other hand, there are individuals who are challenged not because they do not know the direction of their lives, but because they are pulled in a million different directions. Every day you wake up, you are chasing a new vision, dream, purpose, or idea. You are starting a new adventure all of the time, but then you are lost because you don't know which journey you should take.

Whether you are the person who is uncertain of where you are heading, or you are the individual who is traveling down one too many journeys at a time, I encourage you to allow God to order your steps. It is important to use the G.P.S (God Protection Services) when navigating the direction of your future. If you are not led by God, you may take the wrong turn, come to a dead end, or have to reroute the destination. Allowing God to lead you will save you from running out of energy, taking unnecessary U- turns, missing exits, or getting stuck in traffic jams of life. Rid yourself of independence so that you can be led by God. He knows how to navigate our lives better than we can ever hope to.

Release the steering wheel. Believe in the Word of God as it says in Psalm 119:133: "Order my steps according to Your

Word." God is trying to order your steps, so do not stand in the way. Today, I ask that you climb out of the driver's seat and trust God enough to get into the passenger seat as you are led in a divine direction. Sometimes we look around at our lives and ask, "Lord what are you doing? Where are you?" We may see that life is going in a different direction from what we imagined, so we begin to search for answers and clarity. Please know that you are right where God wants you. Buckle up for the journey ahead.

Know that He will get you to your destination of passion, purpose, and vision safely. Hold tight and have faith in the journey. He sees dangers before they even approach you and His driving record in your life is the proof. Pray to give up control in your life, family, friends, finances, and your future. Allow God to navigate you in the direction that is appointed for you, in ALL areas of your life.

Prayer: Lord, I ask that I not get distracted by the redirection of my life. Lord, I want to be a passenger led and guided by Your Holy Spirit. Even when things do not go as planned, I ask that I trust Your direction for my life. Keep me focused on the mission and purpose. Continue to allow my destination to be ordained by You. Protect me from unnecessary U- turns, dead ends, and dangers, seen and unseen. I trust You, Lord. Amen.

CHRISTIAN S. BROWN

Day 5

"No Stressing and Praying"

Scripture: Matthew 11:28

Stressing and praying do not complement one another. When you are going through a season where many situations, people, or things bring you worry or anxiety, you must bring it to the Lord. When we bring things to God, we acknowledge His strength and His omniscient power - the ability to know all in our lives. The Word declares us to, "Come to him, all you who are weary and burdened, and I will give you rest" (Matthew 11:28). When you pray about the things you are being overwhelmed about, it does your spirit no good to continue to harbor those stressors. Learn to let go and let God.

Imagine if you went around saying that you are halfway born again, or halfway a Christian, or halfway human. It would sound either comical or confusing. In that same vein, it should draw attention to our spirits when we possess half-faith or halfway believe in the power and authority of God. We must come to a point in believing that our faith is all or nothing. You must pray and have faith in the words of your mouth and the meditations of your heart, knowing that God hears and sees all, even in the chaos of our lives. There is indeed no job too messy for God to clean up. Today I declare that you will not be one who operates on the half-and-half principle: one dose of stress coupled with a dose of faith. Be fully committed in faith as you pray and release things to God. It's time to build the core of your beliefs in God.

Life is unpredictable. The unexpected occurrences of life can distract our spirits, but continue to have faith anyhow. Strive to allow your prayers and the voice of God to be louder than any worry, unfortunate situation, or shortcoming in your life. In this spiritual journey, you get out what you put in. I pray that you put into your spirit that which will only make it stronger, wiser, and more equipped to handle the stressors of this world. Do you need to clear out certain people, habits, or environments? Do what it takes to get right with God.

When you pray, give it to God. Release control of the situations and exercise faith in your outcomes. No more praying and worrying in the same breathe. Do not insult God in that way. He can handle it even when we cannot. Always remember that prayers are answered even if they aren't answered in the way that we desire. Perhaps what we are praying for is for another season. It may be a delay rather than a denial, or it may not be a part of God's blueprint for our life at all. Trust the decisions of God, knowing that He knows and sees all, and only desires the best for you. No more stressing and praying. It is total faith or nothing at all.

Prayer: Lord, teach me to rid myself of stress, perfection, and worry. Allow me to trust Your plans and Your way for my life. I ask that I increase in my faith and decrease in worrying because I trust You, Lord. I place my life in Your hands today. No longer will I try to be in control, handling a load that was never meant for me to carry. I love You, Lord, and I have faith in Your power. In Your name I do pray. Amen.

Day 6

"You are Somebody"

Scripture: Psalm 139:14

Today, acknowledge that you are different; that the greatest duplication you could ever make is that of your own self because *You are Somebody*. In the frantic search to locate just who we are, we sometimes get lost in self-discovery. We may find ourselves living in the tension of who the world desires for us to be instead of the desires of God. Remember, you have an allegiance to the authority of God and not the world. No one else defines you but God!

No matter the age of life, we are all faced with a moment that make us feel inadequate. Whether it be our age, financial reality, relationship status, or passions of life. This moment causes us to compare ourselves to others - opening up room for jealousy, pressuring many with the desires to obtain an identity that was never meant for them to possess. There is nothing more detrimental than chasing the shadow of another being and not simply believing in the power of your own. Learn to be authentically you today.

Psalm 139:14 declares, "I am fearfully and wonderfully made". Made with great care and intentionality that causes you to have your own identity in a world of over seven billion people. Yes, your own identity! We are all made in the image of Christ, the one of love, peace, and adoration. Therefore, if God is loving and patient, and possesses marvelous power, and authority, so do you. Own the power you possess and remember that you are God's prized possession. Be unapologetically confident in your identity in Christ. Be bold and fearless.

Today, make a conscious decision to fall in love with just who you are, flaws and all. Rid your mind of your imperfections and focus in on what you can offer the world. You were placed here in this world for a reason. Instead of focusing on your weaknesses, let's ponder on your strengths. What are you talented in? What are the gifts that God has placed inside of you? What sets you apart from others and how will you own your differences?

The world awaits to be blessed by your presence. I believe in you and challenge you to have faith to achieve what it is that God has for you because *You Are Somebody*. You are a child of God with endless possibilities ahead. Walk in your authority and let no doubt or doubter hinder you.

Prayer: Lord, I ask that You free me to keep my eyes stayed on You, instead of others around me. I am enough. I choose to accept myself, flaws and all. Lord, I desire to be like no one else but myself, so give me the faith to be the best me that I can be. I am made in Your image; therefore I am a prized possession. Allow me to remember this truth every day of my life. Thank you for loving me exactly as I am, Lord. Amen.

CHRISTIAN S. BROWN

Day 7

"Waking up Your Dreams"

Scripture: Ephesians 5:14

Sleep is a response of the body to refuel and energize for another day. If one gets too much sleep, it leaves the body feeling drained and in need of more energy. What happens when you sleep on your dreams and overextend the dormant state of dreaming? Your dreams begin to lose its momentum and get tossed to the side, forgotten, never reaching a stage of action. Today make the conscious decision to *Wake up Your Dreams*. No longer will they remain a figment of your imagination because you will invite the Holy Spirit into your plans. Today you will be led according to the will of God and not your own.

Today, reflect on the authority that the Lord left behind, an authority that lives within all of us. Activate that authority. Let us begin a journey of actions toward your passions and purposes of life. Many of your dreams may have died, but Ephesians 5:14 declares for you to, "Wake up sleeper, rise from the dead, and Christ will shine on you." *Let's Rise and Shine* so that the light of Christ may be illuminated through you! Ponder on the things that have been passionately placed on your spirit. What is that thing that keeps you up at night? What is that effort you can see yourself doing for eternity? Then listen to the voice of God, who will be your guiding protection along the journey. It may take time to hear the voice clearly, but time and investment yields results.

No more sleeping and dreaming; it is time to *Wake up Your Dreams*. It is time to actively walk toward the purposes and passions that only you can uniquely fill. You were created with a purpose and the world is waiting for you to fulfill it in a mighty way. Creation would not be the same without you. As God's creation, know that God has already placed the tools within you that will activate your future. Thank the Lord that you do not have to go on a search for the power, everything you need is within you already. Nor do you need to borrow it from someone else, because God desires for you to use your own gifts, instead at marveling and using that of others. Today I ask that you acknowledge both your strengths and weaknesses, and use this awareness to your advantage.

Do not be afraid to rise from your sleep and move forward. Know that you can, will, and shall walk in your purpose because you have made the conscious decision to wake up.

Prayer: Lord, wake me up to my passions and purpose. It is impossible for me to do this on my own, so I ask that I hear Your voice, so that I may move forward. You have placed something powerful in me - gifts, talents, and uniqueness - so please allow me to use this to change the world around me. It will not be easy, so give me the strength, Lord. My dreams will no longer be dormant because my faith has been activated. I am awake and alive in You. No longer will I sleep on my future. Thank You for Your guidance. In Your name I do pray. Amen.

Day 8

"Beyond the Fear of Failure"

Scripture: *Joshua 1:9*

Many of us have not reached our highest potential in Christ because we are afraid to fail. There are many places that God desire for us to go, people to touch, lives to witness to, and cycles to break, but we are afraid to take the initial step toward the path that is ordained for us. Oftentimes we are presented with the question, "What will other people think of me?" and "What if I don't succeed?" We are also bound by generational cycles or the failure of others, making them our own, when God has so much more in store. Instead of being afraid to chase after all that God has for you, I ask that today you release yourself from the bondage of the "what if's" and simply live a life of obedience. Dream big!

Many of us can recall the moment we first started to ride a bike. It was a very exciting moment, and yet it brought much anxiety and fear because of the possibility of falling down. We eagerly got on to the bike, overcoming any fear, and tried to balance ourselves so that we could propel into new destinations. Just like this journey called life, you must hop unto the vehicle that God is using to get you to the next destination. Yes, there may be moments when you fall down and inherit a scar, but know that just like riding a bike, you can dust yourself off and get back up again. Your scars only serve as a reminder of the healing power of God. So don't focus on the pain; focus on the destination that your pain is propelling you to. Let's rise beyond the fear of failure.

Life is filled with unknowns, so putting ourselves out there takes vulnerability. What if we fail? What if we are rejected? What if no one understands? Those questions of fear and doubt may come, but you must not stop there. Joshua 1:9 declares, "Be strong and courageous. Do not be afraid; do not be discouraged." Activate your faith, trusting in the power and direction that God has over your life. We may not always get it right, and we may not have all the answers, but when you place your trust in God, you acknowledge that it is for Him to know, not you.

Today, be released from past hurts, fears, or failures that hinder you from reaching your maximum potential. I ask that you do not let one closed door hinder you from knocking and asking God to open another. Do not allow fear to hinder you from your opportunity to bless others through your mighty testimony. Today, I ask that you ponder on the things that have been placed on your heart, big or small, and have the faith that if God call you to it, He will see you through it. You are more than equipped, so stop looking into the past and move forward beyond the fear of failure.

Prayer: Dear Lord, I acknowledge that I am somebody with a purpose and calling. I know that I may not always get it right, but Lord, You are not expecting me to be perfect. I ask that I move beyond my flaws and activate my faith. Give me the strength to do what You have called me to do, beyond my self-doubt and the things of my past. I know I can do it, Lord. I will not be defeated by the spirit of failure. In Jesus' name I pray. Amen.

Day 9

"Small Things Matter"

Scripture: *Matthew 17:20*

Did you know that the small things in life matter? In Jonah 4:1 it reads, "God appointed a worm when dawn came the next day and it attacked the plant, and it withered." You may be wondering, how did an insect so small in size successfully attack an enormous plant? The answer is simple: small things have the power to make a mighty impact. We oftentimes underestimate the consequences of a simple decision, a one-time event, a careless joke, or a "you only live once" attitude. The truth is that the small things can have a huge impact on our lives. Just like the plant, we may find ourselves withering because we are not paying attention to the small temptations, people, or decisions. So today, I pray that you understand the importance of all things, big or small.

Just like the worm, you must focus on your task at hand. I am not boasting in the destruction that the worm caused to the plant. Rather I am putting the emphasis on the determination and obedience of the worm. God appointed the worm just like He has appointed you to do great and mighty things. I pray that you do not focus on the size of the task. Instead have a spirit of fearlessness and obedience. Sometimes we may feel small or insignificant, and we look around at the world and it seems to be so giant. We get it in our head and hearts that we will never have the capacity to do what God has appointed us to do. What if I am not strong enough or the most qualified? What if I am not talented enough? How will people perceive me if I did this thing? There will always be questions and some insecurities along the journey, but do not focus on your size; focus on the task. Mustard seed faith is what is required of you in this season. Read Matthew 17:20.

Small things matter! Today, I pray that you start to work carefully through your speech and actions. I pray that you begin to consult God not just on big decisions for your life, but also small things. It is vitally important to see value in all things, people, and judgements because it all yields to a greater outcome. Just like when we take a break from working out, you may not instantly see a difference in your weight but when you innocently eat one little thing here and there, those small decisions begin to build up and have a greater impact over time. Or how about when you make a small purchase that later has an enormous effect on your bank account? We are to treat all decisions with seriousness. I pray that you become prayerful in your interactions with others and yourself, while being mindful of how your small decisions and actions may affect your future greatly.

Prayer: Lord, I pray today that You allow me to see the value in all things and people, Lord. I ask that I do not underestimate the things in my life. Lord, I pray that I consult with You in all that I do and have a spirit of obedience as I move forward in You, God. Amen.

Day 10

"Write it Down"

Scripture: Habakkuk 2:2

Too often we have desires for our future, but they do not make it past our own imagination. In order for anything to blossom into fruition, it must be watered by action and faith. The first step toward fulfilling anything is to write it down with authority and faith. The Word of God in the Book of Habakkuk 2:2 directs us to, "Write down the revelation and make it plain, so that a herald may run with it." A herald is a person that does not sit still, but one who runs - a person of action. Today I pray that you write down the passions of your heart so that the Holy Spirit may run with them.

In order to write your goals down, it is imperative to understand the difference between an earthly vision and a spiritual vision. An earthly vision is measured by that which you can see using your eyesight. A spiritual vision takes faith to activate because it is impossible to see it using your earthly sight. While you write down your passions, use your spiritual sight as you imagine those things that may not be seen here on earth, but can be manifested spiritually because of the goodness of God. Your earthly sight may be saying that you are not educated enough, financially stable enough, confident enough, that you're too old or young, but know that when using your spiritual sight, God shows you that all things are possible. Dream big. Do not place limits on what you write down because we serve a limitless God.

When you stick God in a box, you also place your dreams and possibilities in there. Today, I ask that you go beyond the sight that is before you in order to look into the next level of your life. Do not look around at your current situation and count yourself out for a spiritual elevation in God, because God controls all things, including the things that you write down. Write down whatever is on your heart – maybe it's that business, that exam, organization, marriage, or person you must forgive; maybe it's that addiction or temptation; maybe it's something else that is tugging at your heart. Whatever it is, make it plain so that you may seek the things that God has for you. What will you write down to achieve in your life? Do not be afraid or discouraged because you have everything that it takes.

Prayer: Lord, give me the courage to write down the goals, passions, and desires of my heart. Whatever is hindering me from getting to the place that You desire for me to be, I ask that You remove it, Lord. When I write down the vision, I ask that You will guide me on what to do next, Holy Spirit. Give me the strength to overcome my earthly sight in order that I may cast a spiritual vision for my life. In Your name I do pray. Amen.

Day 11

"The Prayerful Leader"

Scripture: 1 Thessalonians 5:17

We are all leaders in our unique and specific ways because a true leader does not require a title or position. A wise man once told me that you should never lead anyone without a prayer life. Many individuals want to lead others, but they will do so inefficiently because they are leading themselves instead of being led by the Holy Spirit. Before you ask God for the elevation in your life you must ask yourself, "Am I spiritually sound to lead His people?" Ultimately, you are to reflect upon your prayer life. Leadership incorporates various qualities of character. However, oftentimes individuals forget the essential obedience of being led by the Holy Spirit through prayer. A leader who prays is a leader who is after God's ways. How is your prayer life?

It is important to rid yourself of the notion of there being a "perfect prayer." A prayer is an intimate conversation with God that is free from perfection. The words offered during prayer are utterances from your heart to the ear of God. Start somewhere and do not get discouraged. Unlike the world, God is not here to judge us. He only desires to have a relationship with us. Just like in many earthly relationships, whether in friendships or romantic ones, people say that communication is so important. If this is true, we must not be afraid to communicate in our relationship with God through prayer. If the communication has already begun in your life, it can be strengthened. If it has not begun, today can be your start.

A leader must be a prayerful leader; one who moves according to the leadership of God. Discernment and guidance are achieved through prayer, and these are some of the greatest attributes for a strong leader. Today, I ask that you have a talk with Jesus, and that you acknowledge the importance of praying without ceasing. Allow God to direct your speech, decisions, character, and influence on others. You lead others successfully when you can be led by Christ, so remember that this journey is not your own. Whisper in God's ear today. Allow the voice of the Lord to speak back to you. Take heed to what is being said to you so that you can lead yourself, team, community, family, friends, and colleagues in the way that God desires. In 1 Thessalonians it reminds us to, "Pray without ceasing", and I ask that you make this a priority in your daily routines of life.

Prayer: Lord, I come to You today asking that You strengthen my prayer life, so that I may lead Your people according to Your will. I ask that I stand behind Your leadership, not in front. Give me the wisdom to be led by You and the power to hear Your voice as You communicate to me, O God. Allow me to thirst for prayer and communication with You. Guide me as I become a prayerful leader in You. In Your name I do pray. Amen.

Day 12

"Uncrushable"

Scripture: 2 Corinthians 4:8

A believer of Christ must understand the importance of pressure. In order to get oil from an olive, you must know how to press it with the right pressure, knowing that if it is pressed with too much force, the olive will be crushed. God is aware of the same with you, knowing just the right amount of pressure to use with you in order to get the goodness out. There are situations, people, or circumstances that will come your way. It is important to remember that they are not there to destroy you, but to get the very best out of you. Embrace the pressure and leave the outcomes to God.

Pressure makes diamonds. It is impossible to have the finished stone without it going through a period of cutting and refining before it may be a desired finished product. Just like the pressure used to get oil from an olive, or for a diamond to get its perfect shape, it must go through this metamorphosis stage and so must you. Too often we desire to skip the refining stage in life, but remember just how essential the pressure is to our faith, spiritual growth, and strength. As you endure the rough days or seasons, remember the Word of God declares in 2 Corinthians 4:8, "We are pressed on every side, but not crushed." You may sometimes feel that the pressure of life is suffocating. Stop trying to find a new rhythm of breathing. Instead simply allow God to breathe the breath of life back into you.

In this world, there are many societal pressures. Some people may question your faith and spirituality, but know that God is still working. Remember: what does not defeat you will only make you stronger. Today, I pray that God allows you to build your strength during the refining stages you may face. I pray that you are reminded that, although you feel as if it may crumble you, remember that God is your foundation and He will help you stand. God is pressing a praise and testimony out of you, just like the olive pressed for oil.

The intensity of your life will be used to glorify the Kingdom. You will never know your strength unless you have endured the pressure. You will never know the faithfulness of God if your faith has never been tested. Be strong and mighty today. You have power and authority in the Lord. Look your obstacles in the face today and say, "I am uncrushable."

Prayer: Holy Spirit that lives inside of me, I ask that You grant me strength today. I ask that I am reminded that, when I feel the pressure, Lord, You use the struggle to make me stronger and wiser. Lord, with every press, I will give you praise, knowing that I will not be crushed. Be my foundation and my solid rock. I am strong and mighty in the Lord. Allow me to never forget. Amen.

CHRISTIAN S. BROWN

Day 13

"Stand"

Scripture: Hebrews 10:23

There may be moments when life absolutely brings you to your knees. It may be from personal experiences or from the lives of those around you. No matter the difficulty that you face, remember you are to stand and not fall. Even our most devout men and women of faith in the Bible have moments where they ask if God is even listening. They pray and do not see things manifest, or life may simply hit them so hard that they may question if they are loved by God. The answer is yes, God loves you no matter what you are going through in your life. We are reminded that the weapon may form, but it will not prosper. I pray that you are not defeated today or ever when the weapons in your life appear. I pray that you do not become weak and fearful at adversity, and that you instead stand tall with your feet planted, shoulders squared, and head held up high.

Often times, we view emotions as a sign of weakness. We feel that we do not have the right to utter frustrations, doubt, or misery. The truth is that we are human, which makes us fallible creatures. We worry, we cry, we may even question the happenings of our lives. This shows humanity, not weakness. Although we may find ourselves in such places, I ask that it not be your final place. Instead have faith to rise above whatever obstacle that you may be facing. I do not care how it may shake your faith or if it causes you to question yourself. Just know that with God as your foundation, you shall not fall.

So stand. Stand when the Enemy comes rushing in like a flood. Stand when you do not know where to go or where to turn. Stand when you feel like there is no way out. Stand when you feel like the pressures of the world are causing you to crumble. Remember: as you rise to stand, you are not standing from your strength alone, but from the strength of the Lord.

I do not know the things that you have gone through from your past or present, and I do not know your future. However, I do know that life is filled with twists, turns, and unknowns and that we are not the authors of our lives; that is the duty of God and God alone. So today, be reminded of the strength you receive when you place your hand into the hand of God. Do not go through life feeling lonely. Always remember the vitality found in your relationship with God. Do not be moved by the stressors of life. I pray that you refuse to run in fear as you stand confidently in the power of God.

Today, start to praise your way through hardships, knowing that if you ever fall, God will pick you back up. If you know of anyone who is going through a tough time, I ask that you encourage them by stretching out your hand and helping them to stand. Sometimes we need a helping hand, so don't miss your opportunity to lift someone up. Encourage someone today, and may you be blessed in the Lord.

Prayer: Oh God, sometimes life hits us, and it hits us hard. I ask that today, I do not focus on the difficulties. May I instead be reminded of the strength and power that I possess in You. Lord, I ask that You increase my faith in You. Help me carry the load, Lord. I ask that I be a light unto others. Amen

Day 14

"Trust God Even When You Can't Trace God"

Scripture: Deuteronomy 31:6

There are moments where you may not feel the presence of God. You may look around at the happenings of your personal life or look around at the world, and not understand how particular things have occurred. You may even get to the point of asking, "God, where are You?" The answer is simple: He is right there. Through the chaos and calamities of your life, the Lord is present. When things do not go as planned in your personal life, on the job, or in the world, the Lord is right there. He promised in His Word in Deuteronomy 31:6: "He will never leave you nor forsake you." You must remember this truth as you navigate the journey of life.

I believe that every day is a teaching moment. Life is like a class to educate and empower us through the teachings of new lessons in Christ, the Teacher. When you are faced with opposition, ask the Lord, "What class am I sitting in on today? Is it Patience 101, Faith 301, Forgiveness for Beginners, or Introduction to Love?" Everything is a lesson to be learned.

Therefore, when you are troubled and find yourself in need of God, do not view it as punishment. Instead, ask the Lord to reveal what lesson you are to learn from that particular moment. In the midst of that test, you may frustratingly doubt God and ask if He is there. Yes, He is present, teaching you, and rooting for your success in this learning moment. He is asking for you to trust Him even when you can't trace Him.

God promises in the Word that He knows the plans He has for you. Remember that in the height of your adversity or doubt, God is working on your behalf. Trusting God is a difficult task. Oftentimes we'd rather be in control, but God knows us better than we know ourselves. Can you believe that? So exercise your faith by trusting God. Do not curse God when you are lonely or confused. Instead pray for a better spiritual discernment. It is ok to question and dialogue with God; that's the privilege of having a relationship with someone. Take advantage of the conversation and the opportunity to gain clarity and understanding.

Questions help you to seek knowledge. God is your friend and wants the best for you. Even when you can't see Him moving in your life, know that He is working hard for all of His children, not just a select few. Trust the lessons to be learned, trust your strength in the midst of your test, and trust the presence of God in your life. He is right beside you always. Reach out to hold His hand.

Prayer: Lord God, help me to remember that You are near. With every step that I take, O God, I ask that You allow me to feel Your presence, Lord. When I do not feel You, I ask that You draw me near to Your power. Show me how to trust You even when I do not feel You, so that I may know that You are there beside me. Draw me near, Lord, like never before and if I stray away, pull me back into Your loving arms. Amen.

Day 15

"Staying in Character"

Scripture: James 1:19

Since a young age, my mother always taught me to never let anyone or anything get me out of my character. Understanding this principle will help you protect your witness as a believer. The world is a place that desires to assassinate your character and too often, we give others the power and control to destroy character because we are driven by emotion. Jesus teaches us to not be reactionary and the Epistle of James also reminds us: "Be quick to listen, slow to speak, and slow to become angry" (James 1:19). This is a great model to follow when dealing with people, situations, and circumstances that are not the easiest to navigate.

You must strive to listen more and speak less because it is in those quiet, still moments, that we connect to and hear from God. Oftentimes in heated moments, we are led by emotions and not rationality; therefore we do or say things that we later have to apologize for. God should be glorified through your personality; therefore, you are not to conform into an identity that is not authentic to your witness as a follower of Christ. In leadership and as an ambassador for the Kingdom of God, you can always speak your mind in a godly, character-driven way. Try it! Remember, you must be slow to anger, so today we will pray for your emotions and interactions with others. Even road rage!

Take a moment to reflect on your responses to various situations. Ask yourself, "Have they always been pleasing in the sight of the Lord?" Do you allow your speech and actions to compromise your witness, and your character? What are some ways that you may improve your emotional responses? These questions are vital to ponder upon because you are a leader in Christ, and leadership requires professionalism in actions and emotions. Do not let a person, place, or situation dim the light that Jesus has placed in you. Today you will exercise patience, guard your tongue, and be less reactive in your verbal and nonverbal communication.

Prayer: Dear Lord, I acknowledge that I am an imperfect being who is striving to be near Your holy perfection. Today, I ask that You allow me to be conscious of my speech and actions because You have called me to shine my light. Jesus, I ask that I be quick to listen, slow to speak, and slow to anger, so that I do not compromise my character in You. Rest in me, Holy Spirit, and guide my tongue and emotions. In Your name I do pray. Amen.

Day 16

"Praise Through Your Pain"

Scripture: *Psalm 34:1*

There are moments where your pain has overshadowed your praise. Moments where the hurt is so strong that you may even question if God see your tears or hear your cries. But it is imperative to know that it is also in those forbidden moments that you may realize the healing power of Jesus. Focusing only on your pain while abandoning your praise is what the Enemy desires for you to do. Your obstacles want you to channel in on your current feelings but you must not forget the power and authority of God that can transform that pain into praise.

For a brief moment, think over your life and where the Lord has brought you from and delivered you out of. Ponder on how God has blessed you undeservingly or how you have been protected even when you did not utter a word. Yes, God deserves all of the praise because of the things done in the past and what can be done for your present and future. Today, I ask that you praise through your pain. If pain is not applicable to you today, I ask that you think of someone who may be going through a very painful time in their life. Remind them and yourself to be encouraged in the Lord at all times, even through the undesired moments of life. It is unfair to only praise God after you have been delivered out of pain, so give the Lord glory on today for the goodness and mercy showered into your life.

Praise God in your unique way and confuse the Enemy. The pain is known to place limitations on you or prohibit you in many ways, but a praise a day will keep the Enemy away. Speak that you will no longer be bound by negative thoughts and sadness because you have chosen to praise differently. The Word says in Psalm 34:1: "I will bless the Lord at all times, His praise shall always be on my lips." Therefore today open your mouth and give the Lord praise and honor. Praise the Lord through your pain and misfortunes. Send up praises despite how it looks around you, knowing that God is a healer and that there is no pain that God cannot heal. Trust the process and even the pain, for the Lord's strength is strong and mighty. May any pain of your mind, body, and spirit be given to the Lord.

Prayer: Dear Lord, I thank You for the ability to praise through my pain. I thank You for the strength and endurance that You have placed inside of me. Lord, You grant me with new mercies each and every day, so I will focus on the many ways that I may praise You for all of Your goodness in my life. Lord, I trust that You can heal those painful areas of my life and I will praise You in advance for who You are. Today, I will encourage myself and others to praise You through every season of our lives. In Your name I do pray. Amen.

Day 17

"Forgiveness"

Scripture: Luke 23:24

We all can recall a person or situation that hurt us to the core. It may have been done or said subtly or overtly, knowingly or unknowingly. Nonetheless it made an imprint on your heart and mind. Some of the imprints have left scars over time. Scars in need of healing by our savior, Jesus Christ, while other scars have been tossed away in the sea of forgetfulness. But what about that very thing we can't let go of? It is the thing that controls our reality and emotions, our destiny and fruitfulness; that which keeps us captive in our spirits, unable to get free. I know that we all have journeyed this road before, whether with a family member, friend, significant other, co-worker, neighbor, or acquaintance. Today, I am asking God to give you a forgiving heart so that your healing may begin. Today, I pray that you will begin to adopt the mindset of a forgiver.

Many people of faith believe that forgiveness happens instantaneously; that you wave God's magic wand and your memories, hurt, pain, and turmoil are erased forever. Truthfully, the journey to forgiveness is a process. Never compare your journey to forgiveness with someone else's journey because we are all different, therefore we process and analyze things with varying perspectives.

Forgiveness will rid you of the heaviness in your heart, and the anger and animosity that surfaces from time to time. It will allow you to spread your wings to soar to the highest heights. Emotionally, you may find yourself harboring resentment while the person that has harmed you is enjoying his or her life. You deserve happiness too, so go and get it. This is a serious journey and at times you may feel that this task is impossible, so I invite you to pray to God about who you can choose to journey with you. Inform that person of your goal and allow them to hold your hand in this process. You don't have to do this alone.

You may be asking why you should forgive someone who has hurt you mentally, physically, or spiritually. The truth is that we hurt God daily and yet He grants us mercy and forgiveness daily. Jesus is the greatest model for us and in Scripture, He forgave many people, even the ones who killed him. While on the cross, being tormented by those who wanted him dead, he spoke, "Father, forgive them, for they know not what they do" (Luke 23:24). He still forgave the sins of others. He loved us so much that He died in order for us to live more abundantly. That is what forgiveness looks like.

You deserve to be free, but past hurts keep you bound. May God fill your heart not with anger, but may He fill it with love—a love that will allow you to forgive your enemies even in the midst of healing. Just like Jesus rose after they killed him, you too, may have died in spirit because of a hurt, but you will rise like the eagle and soar to a new level of joy and happiness in your life. Ask God for direction. Remember that throughout this journey, speak things into existence as if it is so. You will be victorious. Repeat: "I will forgive."

Prayer: Dear Lord, I do not wish to carry burdens with me throughout my life. Today, I want You to soften my heart so that I may exercise forgiveness. Lord, I want You to hold my hand during this process, and give me the strength to do what is best for me - to forgive. God, protect my heart and be my foundation in this journey. Amen.

Day 18

"Free from Fear"

Scripture: Psalm 23:4

Many people in this world are afraid to reach their full capacities because of the fear and vulnerability that it may require. Fear is debilitating. It will cause you to be stagnant even when you know that the Lord is calling you to do greater things. God has placed every tool inside of us that is needed to transform the world, but we allow fear to keep us bound and afraid to step out on faith. Today, I pray that you will be fearless and bold to the assignment that God has placed on your heart and mind.

If you do not succeed in your initial attempt, you must dust yourself off and get back up to finish the race given to you. The Lord does not promise there will be no setbacks (also known as lessons learned to strengthen your endurance), but what the Lord does promise is that He will never leave you nor forsake you. Stand on the Word of God as you proclaim to fear no evil, knowing that God is with you. You are powerful beyond measure; the Lord sees it and it is time for you to acknowledge it as well. Some of the most influential people in the Word of God are individuals who understood the power of being fearless. When God called them to make a difference in the world, their obedience was tied to the breakthrough of others just like yours. The world is waiting for you to be fearless, so what are you waiting for?

Being fearless does not mean an absence of doubt, but the presence of faith. Faith knows that God will equip the call that has been placed in your life because if He calls you to it, He will see you through it. Your obedience to overcome your fear will save, motivate, encourage, and empower people both near and far. Rid yourself of perfectionism. The reality is that we will not have all of the answers or know the direction that the Lord is taking us. All that is required is an obedient and fearless heart. Today, I pray that you divorce your fear and marry your faith in order that you may activate the passions and purposes placed inside of you. Lord, if you lead me, I will follow.

Prayer: Dear God, today I ask that any fears and hindrances in my life be made known. I pray on today that I live fearlessly in You, trusting in the gifts that You have placed inside of me. Lord, I pray that I am obedient to You, and that I am reminded that You are with me every step of the way. It is impossible for me to be fearless without You, so I thank You for Your presence in my life. Continue to guide me, O Lord, and do not allow me to be afraid of my own light. Let me shine, O God. Amen.

Day 19

"Agape Love"

Scripture: Romans 8:38

The center of our faith in Christ is love. God is not only concerned by the deeds of your life; He also wants to know the condition of your heart. Many of us are willing to help, lead, and direct others toward Christ and outwardly it looks amazing. However, sometimes when we do a heart-check, we may find that our motivations are not borne from pure love. Today, I ask that you focus on what it means to display the love of Christ - the love of Christ in all settings, situations, and scenarios regardless of whether it is desired or undesired.

Oftentimes, we feel that particular people are undeserving of our love, maybe because of their lifestyle, beliefs, wrongdoings, or treatment of us. It is easy to harbor anger in our hearts, unwilling to love unconditionally, but we all fall short of the Glory of God. Jesus died on the cross for our sins despite how He was mistreated here on this Earth. He fulfilled the will of God and was nailed on the cross, enduring pain and misery, and He did it not because we were perfect or even deserving, but because He loved us. This love displayed was not an ordinary kind of love, but an *agape* love, meaning an open and authentic love. We are to challenge ourselves in showing this same love to others.

We are reminded in Romans 8:38: "Nothing can ever separate us from God's love." As followers of Christ, we are to operate in this Godly love, displaying it to both our friends and foes, not because it comes naturally, but because God has called us to higher standards of loving others.

Truthfully, some of us are apprehensive about loving others due to the love that we have received in our lives. Some have delighted in the actions of love while others may have been hurt in the name of love. When considering our experiences in our families, friendships and churches, the idea of love can be filled with both good and bad recollections. Yes, earthly love is complicated, but the spiritual love of God is incomparable.

God cares about you so much that in Luke 12:7, it says: "The very hairs on your head are numbered." He is patient in His love. God loves you so much that He grants you grace and mercy daily, forgiving you, and giving you a second chance even when it is undeserved. He loves us in our mess and in our flaws, through our neglect of Him and even in our withdrawals. Despite all, God blesses us with life and the opportunity to get it right, and that is nothing but love.

In Acts 20:25 the Word of God proclaims, "It is better to give than to receive." So don't go looking just to receive love today; give it to someone else. Let someone know how much you care, or let the Holy Spirit lead you on how you can show love to someone. It is *agape* love that will transform the culture of this world. This transformation can begin with your unconditional love for others. Love on someone today!

Prayer: Dear Lord, I pray that You allow me to walk in Your love. As I am surrounded by Your love, I ask that I am able to show this same love to others. I ask that I am not judgmental of those around me and that I offer grace, just as You offer it to me. I declare that *agape* love will be the foundation of my very being, and that You will guide my interactions with others. In Your name I do pray. Amen.

Day 20

"Relationships"

Scripture: Job 1:21

There are many moments when we are faced with the reality that some people are not as close to us as they used to be. This reality can be disheartening, overwhelming, and disappointing. We may recall when a particular person was a priority in our lives, only to find that God had other plans. When dealing with people, one of the most important things we can learn about relationships - whether romantic, friendly, spiritual, or professional - is that some people are placed in our lives for a season while others are placed in our lives for eternity. Only time and communication with God will allow us to know the difference.

Today, open your heart and mind to healing from a broken relationship that is hindering you so that you can move forward. I pray that you understand that some relationships are not intended to stay around forever. Although this may be shocking, trust the Lord with who He allows to access you. It is time to heal from the hurt of your past and move into your destiny.

As you grow and mature into who God has called you to be, He will allow people to cross your path who may assist you to the next level. Imagine when you were in grade school and you were introduced to a teacher for only one year. After the teacher has taught you everything you needed to know in that level of your learning, you then had to move on in order to reach the next grade. Similarly, God allows certain people in at various levels of our lives to help us mature, learn, and become better individuals. This may be emotionally or spiritually draining, but God always has our best interest at heart. As you travel in purpose, you must acknowledge that everyone around you is not meant to stay on the train with you. We all have various destinations in life and only the chosen ones in your life will ride it to the very end. As God removes some individuals from your life, know that He will be introducing you to more people. Keep an open heart and mind to all you come in contact with, guarding your heart always.

When we lose people in our lives, we may give too much credit to the enemy. We are to be reminded in Job 1:21: "The Lord giveth and the Lord taketh away." Have you ever thought that God has taken away a relationship for your protection? He loves you so much that He protects you from all hurt and danger both seen and unseen. New elevations call for new relations, so trust the plan of God. Regain control, we give others too much power.

I pray that today, you will find peace, knowing that God will only allow you to grow with those who will pray for you and not prey on you. Acknowledge that every relationship that has ended did not end because of anger, deceit, or deception, but simply because your time with that person has innocently run out. No matter how it ended, we must spiritually trust why it did. Have faith that God has control, even when we personally lack control in our relationships. Keep your head up. Don't be defeated as God continues to shift the people in your life. Look forward and do not look back in the past.

Prayer: Dear God, I pray that You heal me to move forward from certain people. I ask that You heal me, and empower me to trust You enough to determine who enters and leaves my life. Lord, keep me shielded and protected. Teach me to look forward, not to the past. God, thank You for allowing me to know all the individuals in my life, whether seasonal or long-term. In Your name I do pray. Amen.

CHRISTIAN S. BROWN

Day 21

"Waiting for the Appointed Time"

Scripture: *Habakkuk 2:3*

You must know that everything has an appointed time to be released if you are wanting to walk in the vision that God has placed on your heart. Habakkuk 2:3 declares, "For the revelation awaits an appointed time", so be patient in your waiting. If we walk into particular doors, jobs, promotions, or relationships prematurely, we will abuse the blessing and lose what God has for us. Therefore we must have patience. For a moment, ponder on the things that you are asking God for in your life. Think about the things that keep you up at night and what you pray for. Now ask yourself if you are spiritually mature enough to handle all that God is going to bless you with. With new levels comes new devils, and with new blessings come new enemies who will come to get you off course.

Just like the growth of a baby, everything has a process. If birthed too soon, it may be premature. This same reality applies to your dreams and passions if they are birthed too soon, complicating the vitality of the vision. Therefore, it is essential that you wait for the appointed time for your visions and dreams to be birthed. Pray that God's will be done and not your own. Patience is essential to the growth of an individual. So today, I pray that the Lord grants you patience as you await your appointed time. This is not only applicable to your vision in life, but it has relevance as you may await a job, relationship, healing, finances, and so on.

Remember that a delay is not a denial. So do not count yourself out just because something did not manifest at a particular hour. Remember, "It may not come when you want it, but it'll be there right on time." Yes, that is accurate. While you wait, know that God is working. After all, it is important for you to exercise faith, which is known as the substance of things hoped for and the evidence of things not seen. Believe that God has your best interest at heart, including timing. Ask God to reveal what you are to do in your life, and then await the revelation knowing that it has its appointed reveal. Trust the purpose-filled process.

Prayer: Dear Lord, this day I ask that You allow me to not only discover my passion, but that I have the patience to wait for it to be manifested in its appointed time. Things do not happen instantaneously, so I ask that I neither give up on You nor myself as I await You, Lord. Allow me to keep my faith and perseverance in this journey. In Your name I do pray. Amen.

CHRISTIAN S. BROWN

Day 22

"Turning the Other Cheek"

Scripture: Luke 6:29

As believers, we might ask the question, "Why do I have to always be the bigger person?" This question more than likely comes from great frustration and confusion because it is a very difficult calling in the heat of confrontation. We live in a world where your patience will always be tested. Those tests come in many forms. The more that you work for the Kingdom of God and lead His people, in your family, on the job, in school, the more you will be attacked to be destroyed. As a leader, you must not seek payback or revenge. Instead you are to operate in love and forgiveness daily. That boss, family member, store clerk, neighbor, or enemy may be deserving of your revenge, but remember that you are to shine the light of God at all times in your speech and actions, especially when being tested. This is not weakness; it is wisdom.

Jesus shined the light of God in all that He did. He was always seen doing the right thing, helping, healing, preaching, and being an advocate for the oppressed. Due to His positive contributions to society, He was a sought after individual in the Bible because of His good deeds. People always tested Jesus' righteousness and they will do the same to you. Just like Jesus, you may be one striving to do the right thing and somehow the Enemy sends someone to test your patience. Stand strong and allow the Holy Spirit to be your guide. Treating evil with evil will only aggravate the issue. Therefore you must decrease flesh and allow the Holy Spirit to rest upon you. Easier said than done, but you can do it if you give it a try.

Today, I ask that you become less reactionary and more Spirit-led. Call on the name of the Lord when the Enemy comes to destroy you. You are made in the image of God and your actions must reflect that. Do as the Lord has instructed in Luke

6:29: "If someone slaps you on one cheek, turn to them the other also." Do not dwell on wrongdoings. Allow God to be the disciplinarian in life. Do not take matters into your own hands; consult with God. If you fear losing control, walk away knowing that this is not a sign of weakness but a sign of spiritual maturity.

I thank God in advance for your new responses to moments of adversity. Decrease your flesh and allow the Spirit to lead you. Turn the other cheek and walk away, it's not worth compromising your spirit. May you have a blessed and prosperous day, child of God.

Prayer: Holy Spirit, I ask that You rest in me today like never before. I want to be like You when I respond to people and things that upset me and I acknowledge that I need Your help to do it. As a believer, I want to learn how to turn the other cheek and respond using wisdom instead of emotions. This is not a weakness, but it is wise, O Lord. I thank You for allowing me to be more like You. In Your name I do pray. Amen.

CHRISTIAN S. BROWN

Day 23

"Show up"

Scripture: *Deuteronomy 31:8*

While getting to know someone, or during the phase of dating, one of the most damaging things someone can do is stand you up. For most people, this sends their blood boiling. Some people may promise to never contact the person again, others may have grace to ask and seek answers, while there are those who may view it as karma because they have done it before to others with no remorse. In conclusion, standing someone up is a huge no-no!

When God instructs us to go somewhere, whether a job, relocation, relationship, conversation, or any other direction, His spirit is already there before we are ever instructed. Think about something that the Lord has placed on your heart to do or say, and now imagine Him being there before you were ever instructed. God has set a divine date with your destiny and is simply asking you to show up. The Word of the Lord declares in Deuteronomy 31:8: "The Lord himself goes before you and will be with you." Therefore, God is already in the plans and at the places that He desires for us to go, waiting for us to arrive.

When we refuse to follow His directions and fail to show up in disobedience, it is as if we stand Him up. God is there, patiently waiting for you to have the confidence to simply arrive at your destination of life, knowing that He will guide and protect you along the way. God wants nothing but the best for us all and I pray that fear does not hinder you from arriving to the places that God is calling you to in the world, your community, job, school and life. Know that God is there to protect, shield, and guard all of His creation. Especially you!

Today, I pray that you let down your defenses and your guard, so that you can allow the Holy Spirit to lead you. I pray that you have the faith to go to the people, places, and things that God is calling you to courageously. That vision, passion, relationship, job, education, conversation, or dream is all being met by God. In fact, He is already there and is waiting for you to arrive. When you fail to show up to what God is leading you to, it is as if you are standing up both God and your future. Choose to move in obedience today, meeting God there because He is waiting patiently. Go now, trusting in the Lord. It's your season of action.

Prayer: Lord, today I ask that You allow me to get rid of my reservations, so that I may be obedient to where You have for me to go. I trust that You are there before I get there, Lord. All You are asking of me is to have faith enough to show up. Guide me, Lord, and lead me in only the way You can. I desire to show up in the moments You have for me. Thank You for always being there, dear Jesus. Amen.

Day 24

"Increased Attacks"

Scripture: *Ephesians 6:10-11*

When you get closer to your purpose and plans, you will notice something: sometimes a presence comes in like a flood to discourage and distract you. When you make up in your mind that you will live for God, the world becomes even more challenging and you seem to develop increased pressure. When you are living for God and chasing after the plans He has for your life - that is when you upset the Enemy even more. Do not be alarmed that as soon as you get closer to your purpose that attacks from the Enemy become more frequent. Stay in the fight; you are doing something right.

With new levels come new devils, and with promotion comes a need for greater devotion. If you were not a threat to the world, you would not be attacked as much. Consider it a privilege to meet resistance because you are a threat to those who do wrong. Do not look around and compare your tribulations to others because you are different. The Lord knows that you can handle the pressure.

Today, I pray that you not dismiss the attacks on your emotions, finances, family, friendships, or future because it will yield growth. Instead of running or complaining, ask God to give you the strength to fight back, knowing that with God on your side, you can win the battle. God loves you and will see you through any adversity. You may even know someone who is under spiritual attack. I pray today that you can stand in the gap for them and declare their victory. There is no testimony without a test, so fight hard so that God can get the glory.

As you encounter the tribulations of your day, I pray that you choose to not fight this battle alone. Instead put on the full armor of God. Do as the Word instructs us in Ephesians 6:10-11: "Be strong in the Lord and in His mighty power. Put on the full armor of God, so that you can take your stand against the devil's schemes." When you are fighting battles, do not fight them alone. God desires to be there to fight them for you if you allow Him. The armor of God will protect, shield, and empower you more than your strength can do alone. Put on this armor today by spending time with God. Allow Scripture, prayer, faith, and meditation to be your armor and protection. Do not be dismayed at the size of the battle. Instead be astonished at the power of God to defeat any enemy that comes your way today and forevermore.

Prayer: Dear God, I thank You for giving me the strength to fight the battles of the Enemy. I acknowledge that I am unable to fight them alone, so I ask that You provide me with Your full armor of protection, dear Lord. I am somebody and because of this, the world will try to slow me down. I declare victory over my life and the lives of those around me. Give me strength, Lord, and allow your Holy Spirit to comfort me in battle. Amen.

Day 25

"The Power of Words"

Scripture: Proverbs 18:21

There is great power in the words that we use. Words can be used to build something or someone up, and they can also be used to tear something or someone down. As a believer, your word is your bond. Therefore you should be very careful in how you use your speech. Speaking things into the atmosphere has great power. Recall a time when you encouraged someone or gave them a compliment. Do you remember how that made them feel? Now think of a time where your speech and tone was unpleasant, and someone became offended or unappreciative of the words that you spoke. Indeed, words have the authority to shift the atmosphere for better or for worse. As a leader, I pray today that you carefully consider the power and effect that words may have on you and others.

Your job, home, school, finances, or social environments may be undesirable at moments. Instead of elaborating on its shortcomings, speak life into it. Instead of complaining or becoming frustrated, challenge yourself to shift the atmosphere by speaking positively over that which causes you stress, discomfort, or unhappiness. Remember there is power in the tongue! Speak life into the atmosphere, and watch how it shifts your mind and heart. I specifically challenge you to speak positively to individuals who may not be the nicest to you. Difficult people need love and affection, too. So today, I pray that you are able to challenge yourself to release positivity into the world, starting with your speech.

We are reminded in Proverbs 18:21: "Death and life are in the power of the tongue." I declare that you choose life over death. No matter the obstacles that may come your way, understand the power of words. Let the Lord lead you to encourage some young child, a friend, a stranger, or a foe, all by using the power of your words. You truly have endless possibilities for how God can use you to bless others when you are one who speaks life rather than death. If it is difficult for you to speak positively, today challenge yourself to release words of encouragement just once. If you are unable to verbally speak it, call on the Holy Spirit to guide your tongue by giving you the words to say. Today, I declare for you to use your words to empower, encourage, and educate others, acknowledging there will be no more outpouring of negativity.

Speak life!

Prayer: Dear Lord, I pray that You give me the strength to use my words, wisely Lord. I choose today that I will encourage and not offend; empower and not destroy. Allow me to walk up to anyone, and any situation, and use my words mightily and wisely. Holy Spirit, guide my tongue so that it may build up Your Kingdom. Give me the words to speak to Your people, O Lord. In Jesus' name I pray. Amen.

CHRISTIAN S. BROWN

Day 26

"Things Change"

Scripture: Proverbs 3:5

At one point of our lives, we were infants, born into the world with an unexplainable innocence. We could not stay in that helpless state of infancy, so God allowed us to grow and mature into individuals who would comprehend the words that you are reading on the pages of this book. Many times we view change as negative. However, change in our lives is inevitable and unescapable. Knowing that things change may be frightening, so we spend a lot of time hoping and wishing that things and people can go back to the way that they used to be. We fail to remember that the only constant thing in our lives is Jesus Christ, our Lord and savior.

Too often we dwell over things and people of the past, unwilling to yield to the newness that God has placed in our lives. Yes, this newness may come at the cost of relationships or friendships, leaving us to want to continue to hold on to something that has expired. Yet it is pivotal to understand that some things and some people are seasonal. Just as the seasons change, circumstances in our lives change, not to hurt or hinder us. Rather it is designed to make us stronger. Our bodies or minds may change, and it may not be the way that it use to be, but getting older and wiser, experiencing more of the fullness of life, is truly a blessing.

So today, I declare that the Enemy will not allow you to dwell on the changes in your life. Thank God for shifting you instead. As you continue to grow and mature in Christ, always remember that everyone and everything will not elevate with you. Embrace your change of friendships, relationships, jobs, mindsets, and endeavors as you rise in Christ. Trust the journey that God has for you.

Change is great when we desire it, but what happens when God unexpectedly allow things to change? Sometimes we fight the change out of fear. I ask that today, you declare that you will no longer look at change in a negative light, and that you will remember that to change is to gain. When change happens, God grants you the opportunity to experience new adventures, new experiences, and new people. In contrast, the unwillingness to embrace change is stagnation.

Think of some of the people with influence in the Word of God. John the Baptist and his many baptisms, Moses leading the people out of the wilderness, or Jesus dying on the cross; all of these magnificent encounters of strength would not have been manifested if they were afraid of change. So, I pray that you neither dwell in the past nor that you fear change. Truly allow the will of God to manifest in your life.

Prayer: Dear God, I pray that You allow me to be at peace with the shifts that occur in my life. Lord, I ask that You empower me to give up control, so that I may move forward in my destiny. God, allow me to see change in a positive way, so that I may fully live in Your will. Grant me healing over the changes that may cause me some hurt and pain. I know You can give me peace and I thank You in advance. Amen.

CHRISTIAN S. BROWN

Day 27

"Stay Focused"

Scripture: *Hebrews 12:1*

As children, we were often presented with the question, "Who do you want to be when you grow up?" With animated responses, we would name the heroes of our times who had a great impact in our communities and world. We admired their skills, passions, and talents, believing that if we followed their model, we could be just like them and more. Truthfully, the question that should have been posed is "what" you want to be, instead of "who" you want to be. Later in life, we find ourselves pressured to imitate and duplicate others. Since our youth, we have been trained to be like someone else instead of chasing the Someone that is already inside of us. Today, acknowledge your giftedness. Acknowledge that you should not look to the left or to the right at others around you. Instead, stay focused on the person ahead of you, who is Jesus.

In Hebrews 12:1-2, the Word of God proclaims: "And let us run with perseverance the race marked out for us, fixing our eyes on Jesus, the pioneer and perfecter of faith." In this life, there will be much temptation to see others and desire to be like them, or at least to have their same success. The greatest influence of our time is social media, which glamorizes the end product, very seldom scratching the surface of truth. I pray that you begin to live out your truth and not get distracted by who and what is surrounding you.

Today, I ask that you choose to originate, not duplicate. Do not be dismayed at your flaws or shortcomings. Focus instead on the gifts and strengths that God has placed in you since birth. Stop looking around, comparing your journey to others. Run the race that has been marked for you alone, keeping your eyes on Jesus. With your eyes on Jesus, and not man, you will stay focused, motivated and strengthened to endure your race to the end.

The Enemy will use anything to distract and discourage you. Your age, education, finances, health, confidence, friends, school, background or any other obstacle, all to stop you from doing the work of the Lord. He knows your weakness so he will send that very thing or person to steer you off-course. Life can be painful sometimes and you may want to give up, but know that God has already spoken a spirit of perseverance over your life. Keep going.

As you run your race, stay in perfect spiritual posture: head up, eyes focused, heart centered, and energized to run to the end. Let no human tell you who you will become or the places that you may go while running your *own* course, in your *own* lane, according to your *own* timing in God. Keep your eyes set on Jesus and stay focused. You've got this!

Prayer: Dear Lord, I ask that You allow me to not look to the left or right, but that I stay focused on You, O God. Father, allow me to be all that I can be, so that I may give my all to change the world. Lord, I can't do this without You. I thank You for holding my hand along this journey. I have places to go. No matter how difficult the course, give me the strength to run it with endurance and perseverance. I love You, God, and I give Your name all the glory. Amen.

Day 28

"A Divine Interruption"

Scripture: Proverbs 3:5

Oftentimes we map out our next phases of achievement. One of the most hopeful moments in life is when we are able to tell others the places we desire to go in the next few years. It allows you to dream, hope, and believe toward the things that are to come with persistence and dedication. These goals vary amongst individuals, including: starting a family, earning a higher education, retiring, visiting that city you've always dreamed of, or writing that book that has been placed on your heart. I know your dreams and aspirations are endless and sometimes it seems like there is nothing that can stop our imagination in achieving these goals, making them a reality.

But one of the things that shake our faith as believers is when we encounter a divine interruption. When the very things that we list on our hearts do not go as desired. When things do not manifest as we planned and the promises of God have not yet been fulfilled. What do you do? How does your spirit respond? Where do you lie on the spectrum of faith?

The first lesson you learn once you've given up control of your future, allowing God to lead you, is that things do not always go according to your plans. You may have set out for one goal, only to find it delayed or to not come into fruition at all. I pray that today, you accept the divine interruptions that may come your way. No, you are not a failure and no, you are not defeated. It is time to trust in the plans that God has for you, knowing that His way is better than any known way.

Divine interruptions are not setbacks; they are a set up for what is to come in the future. Perhaps there may have been a particular lesson to be learned or a person that you had to meet along your journey, but a detour was necessary to get you there. I pray today that you do not resist the plans of God.

Continue to trust the path, even when it may not be clear.

Do not look at detours and interruptions as anything other than divine. God is very much a part of the "stop," "not right now," and "hold on" moments in your life, just as much as the "yes" moments. You must humbly accept them all. Perhaps when the direction shifts, instead of feeling defeated or frustrated, ask God what is it that He wants you to learn. What has He protected you from? The detours of life are all sacred, whether they are God-induced or human-induced, because detours lead to redirection. We may think we are heading in the right direction with that special vision, relationship, ministry, business, but we may be a little off-course, so God has to reroute our destination.

I pray that today, you look at interruptions as divine interventions from God. I also pray that you are communicating with God enough to know how to handle the detours. Remember: God sends divine interruptions while the Enemy sends distractions. There is a difference! Pray to God to allow you to know the difference, alerting you in mind, body, and spirit as you navigate through your journey.

Prayer: Dear God, I thank You so very much for being the protection in my life, Lord. Allow me to trust Your process, even if things don't go as I desire. Lord, I thank You for the divine interruptions I've encountered. May You forever protect and guide me, all the days of my life. Amen.

.

Day 29

"Praise God in Advance"

Scripture: *Psalm 145:2*

One of the Enemy's greatest weapons is to stop our praise. Sometimes, life will hit us so hard, that we may lose faith and hope in the future. But today, I ask that you not focus on the negativity around you. Instead praise God in advance for your victories. What you speak out into the world is a reflection of your reality in mind, body, and spirit. So start to praise God in advance. Wake up with praise and thanksgiving on your tongue, worshipping God for the small things in your life that you tend to overlook, each and every day.

The Word of God says in Matthew 25:23, "If we are faithful over the few, He will make us ruler of many". Therefore, today begin to give God a mighty praise over what may seem like small blessings in your life. Begin to claim victory despite how circumstances may manifest. Know that you have the victory because you have spoken it. Therefore, it is so.

One of the greatest ways to confuse the Enemy is to give God praise when you are in the pit of your tribulation. The Enemy wants you to be burdened with sorrow and gloom. So when you praise God and give glory to His name, you stifle the Enemy. When people look at you today, I pray that the glory of God shines so brightly that others begin to feel a praise in their spirit, simply from your presence.

We may encounter many difficulties in life, but many of us don't look like what we have gone through. We all endure hardships; therefore, no human on this earth is excused from a testimony. Each of our trials may be packaged differently, nonetheless we have all encountered some struggles. No matter the obstacle, we simply have to praise our way through.

Encourage your spirit today. Walk with your head held high, knowing that God has you covered with the blood.

When you are weak, praise God. When you feel doubtful, praise God. When you feel like there is nowhere to go or turn, praise God. When life is fabulous and you are on the highest cloud in heaven because of favor, praise God. Praise Him in the valley and praise Him on the mountaintop for who He is. Every day that you have breath in your body should be another opportunity to give God glory and adoration for giving you another chance to make a difference in the world. Things may not be the way that you desire them, and life may not be running at the pace you desire, but you are to praise God anyhow. Begin to speak life and not death, and watch how your spirit will lift. I declare nothing but positivity to surround you. May the Lord fill you will love, joy, peace, and praise today.

Prayer: Dear Lord, today I praise You for who You are in my life. I give Your name the honor and glory. Lord, I lift up Your name, and I lift up any difficult situation that I encounter. I will praise Your name, God, no matter what I may be going through. I will not be defeated by the Enemy. I speak life over me and those around me, God. In Your name, I do pray. Amen.

CHRISTIAN S. BROWN

Day 30

"The Shepherd's Voice"

Scripture: John 10:27

You are not leading yourself along this journey called life. You are being led by God. In order to understand the direction that you are being led to, you must be able to hear the voice of the Lord. Understand that this is not an easy task. There are people and circumstances that are fighting for your attention and will try to speak over the voice of God. This distracting voice will have you going places, doing things, and living a life that is not pleasing to yourself or the Lord because it serves as a distraction for you. Be careful about the voices that we listen to in our daily lives.

Today, I pray that you block out all of the noises of your life and that you focus on the only voice that matters, which is God's voice. John 10:27 says, "My sheep listen to my voice; I know them, and they follow me." You have authority because God speaks to you (yes, you!) but you have to know the voice. No longer will you listen to those inner voices that lead you from the path that God desires for you. No longer will you be held captive by the distractions of your life. Pray that the Holy Spirit guide the things and people that you listen to, and that your hearing may be anointed in the name of Jesus.

As the sheep, hearing the voice of the shepherd is imperative for survival. There may be dangers approaching us that we are incapable of seeing, and it is the job of the shepherd to lead the sheep out of harm's way, but the sheep must be led by the voice that guides them. There also may be times when your sight is altered and the direction that God may be taking you is blurry, but hearing the voice of the Lord will serve as the greatest compass for direction and clarity. Do not move until you hear the voice clearly. Be still (and yes, this applies to that business, relationship, tough decision, or conversation). Be led by the voice of God in all that you do.

Remember: the only voice that matters, is of the Lord. Tune out the negative voices of others, even if it is coming from those closest to you. Be encouraged, God wants nothing but the best for you. Listen to the Shepherd's voice and as sheep, do not resist the guidance.

Prayer: Dear Lord, I ask that You grant me the discipline to hear Your voice clearly. I pray that I am able to be guided like the sheep, O Lord. Today, I am praying that You allow my decisions and actions to be made out of my obedience to Your voice and guidance. Allow Your Holy Spirit to guide me as I navigate through this day, freeing me from any noises that may hinder me from moving forward. I will no longer listen to toxic things or people because I will turn to You, God. I pray all these things in Your name. Amen.

Personal Prayers
Section:

1. Find a scripture that speaks to your heart.

2. Write a prayer that relates to this scripture

3. Remember, there is no perfect prayer!!!

Personal Prayers

Scripture:

_____

_____

_____

Prayer:

_____

_____

_____

_____

_____

_____

_____

_____

_____

_____

_____

_____

_____

_____

_____

_____

Personal Prayers

Scripture:

_____

_____

_____

Prayer:

_____

_____

_____

_____

_____

_____

_____

_____

_____

_____

_____

_____

_____

_____

_____

Personal Prayers

Scripture:

_____

_____

_____

Prayer:

_____

_____

_____

_____

_____

_____

_____

_____

_____

_____

_____

_____

_____

_____

_____

_____

Personal Prayers

Scripture:

_____

_____

_____

Prayer:

_____

_____

_____

_____

_____

_____

_____

_____

_____

_____

_____

_____

_____

_____

_____

_____

Personal Prayers

Scripture:

_____

_____

_____

Prayer:

_____

_____

_____

_____

_____

_____

_____

_____

_____

_____

_____

_____

_____

_____

_____

_____

Personal Prayers

Scripture:

_____

_____

_____

Prayer:

_____

_____

_____

_____

_____

_____

_____

_____

_____

_____

_____

_____

_____

_____

_____

_____

Personal Prayers

Scripture:

_____

_____

_____

Prayer:

_____

_____

_____

_____

_____

_____

_____

_____

_____

_____

_____

_____

_____

_____

_____

Personal Prayers

Scripture:

_____

_____

_____

Prayer:

_____

_____

_____

_____

_____

_____

_____

_____

_____

_____

_____

_____

_____

_____

_____

_____

JOIN THE MOVEMENT:

WWW.RISEINCHRIST.COM

FOLLOW US ON INSTAGRAM:
@RISEINCHRIST
@_ CHRISTIANSBROWN

RISE IN CHRIST

Made in the USA
Columbia, SC
27 October 2020

23514440R00083